Carol M
March
God Bless!

LIFE'S JOURNEY

An Inspired Collection of Poetry

To Margaret

Mothers are a blessing
From morning until night
The love that oozes from them
Can be a sheer delight
And we're so very happy
That your love, which we both share
Surrounds us every single day
With tender loving care!

HAPPY MOTHERS DAY!

LIFE'S JOURNEY
An Inspired Collection of Poetry

CAROL McCLENAGHAN

JANUS PUBLISHING COMPANY
London, England

First Published in Great Britain 2002 By
Janus Publishing Company Ltd,
76 Great Titchfield Street,
London W1P 7AF

www.januspublishing.co.uk

Copyright © 2002 by Carol McClenaghan
The author has asserted her moral rights

**British Library Cataloguing-in-Publication Data
A catalogue record for this book
is available from the British Library**

ISBN 1 85756 527 4

Typeset in 11pt Baskerville
By Chris Cowlin

Cover Design William Russell

Printed and bound in Great Britain

CONTENTS

Nature 1
God's Garden 3
The Gentleman's Estate 4
The Park 5
The Beach 7
The Spider 8
Ireland's Countryside 9
Nature's Playground 10
God's Ocean 12
The Old Log Fire 13
Day And Night 15
Earth's Beauty; Heaven's Glory 16

Family and Friends 19
Baptism 21
Our Daughter 22
You Always Put A Smile On My Face 23
Lessons To Be Learnt Though The Life Of A Child 24
Childhood's Eyes 25
Don't Deny Your Children The Gift of God's Creation 27
Your Teddy Bear 29
God's Mansion In The Sky 31
What Is A Mother? 33
Our Parents, Our Best Friends 34
My Husband 36
Age And Youth In Harmony 38
Neighbours 40
Friends Are Like Sunshine 41
Friendship 42

God's Healing Power   43
Share The Good News   45
Do Unto Others, As You Would Have Them Do To You   47
GREED!   49
God Knows What Is Best!   51
Life Is Like A Yo-Yo   53
There Is So Much Competition   54
Slow Down In The Fast Lane   55
Our Province Needs God's Love   57
Jesus Wants To Care For You   59
Celebrate God's Love   61
God's Healing Place For Man   62
The Physician   64
Take Time To Be With God, He'll Ease Your Stressful Load   65
Your Master, Your Lord   67

God's Love For Man   69
God Shows His Love   71
The Trinity   72
Unconditional Love   73
When Trials And Temptations Come   74
Jesus Our Example   75
Our Special Friend   77
God's Gift Of Senses   78
Inner Beauty   80
Your Love, New Life   81
You Are God's Original   82
God's Purpose   83
The Potter's Hand   84
Friends From Distant Shores   86
To Meet With Friends Departed   88
Accept God's Love   89
Who Could Ever Deny God?   90
Jesus, Your Rock, Your Hiding Place   91
Don't Shut God Out   92
Jesus His Purpose To Fulfil   93
God's Presence Through Life's Storms   95

The Rainbow	96
God's Miracles, Yesterday, Today and Forever	98

Speaking With God 101
Commune With God In Prayer!	103
God's Precious Gift Of Life	104
Praise God	105
My Life Your Will	106
Using God's Precious Gifts	108
Fruits Of The Spirit	109
Lord Help Us To Show Your Love	110
Let Me Hear Your Voice, Lord	111
Today I Lost A Friend, Lord	112
Heal The Pain	113
Open Up Our Hearts	114
I Know You Are Always There	115
Telecommunication (Not)	116
Lord Lead Us By Your Guiding Hand	117

Nature

God's Garden

Loving heavenly Father, each day I seek your face
Through nature's glory, created by your amazing grace
The vibrant yellow daffodil, the tulip's bowing head
The pansies, with their smiling faces, align the flower-bed
Buds burst full to blossom, a buzzing bee drops by
A butterfly flits gracefully, as it passes on its way
A spider spins its web of threads, its prey to capture there
Two kittens roll and tumble, they make a playful pair
The sky so blue above me, the clouds a fleece of white
Birds glide swiftly along their path, with feathered wings of flight
From soil each separate blade of grass shoots through, dew dropped at dawn
And mingle with impression to create a freshly mown lawn
Our natural world around us, a purpose to fulfil
Can only be God's blessing, His masterpiece of skill
Our human minds can marvel at how it all combines
Each piece its own intention and uniqueness in design
A reason just for being, a carefully mastered plan
Yet no one could deny, this creativity not of Man
So Lord I bow before you and praise you for your gift
Your natural world's expression, through life's garden beautifully sifts
To gaze out of a window, this beauty vast to see
Provides a meaningful tête-a-tête between both you and me.

The Gentleman's Estate

In a dimly lighted coppice on a Gentleman's estate
A meandering stream its pathway skilfully through woodland navigates
It etches out its form beneath a canopy of leaves
In harmony, nature's artist a masterpiece achieves
A wooden rung bridge stretched across admires the sight beneath
And carries passers-by, its peaceful beauty to proudly reach
Below the water rushes, a melody to the ear
Its cascades effervesce, the sweetest symphony to hear
Some plotted pebbles split its flow, with fleeting flecks of lather
Each bubble fizzles out, a white residue to gather
A bronzed leaf flutters, its bed to lay upon the feathered foam
It glides its path amid the froth, to rest along the loam
A twig drifts weary, the ripples linger to ferry their cargo downstream
The whispering wind, the aqueous quiver and twig form an admirable team
A rugged boulder forms an isle amid the river's flurry
Its oscillating swirl splashes spray at this mountainous form as it hurries
Serenity and tranquil mood envelop all who linger
Pensive, dreamy atmosphere acquired at the click of a finger
Concentration drifts away upon a cloud of peace
Causing worry, stress and tension to automatically decrease
For a moment stopped in time, a concept's given birth
That here we can experience a precious twinkle of Heaven on earth.

The Park

The air resounds with children's laughter, they run and shout with glee
Oh to be a child again, our adults' world to flee
To watch as we recall our childhood days at play
It doesn't seem that long ago, it seems like yesterday
The parks were so much simpler then, we thought we had it all,
A swing, a slide, a roundabout, we kicked around a ball.
But to sit and watch the playtime of our younger generation
Alerts us to a different style of daytime recreation
Those swings and slides and roundabouts have cleverly been revamped,
A park is now comparative to an adventure island camp
The tubular frames are cleverly formed, surrounded by bark or wood chip,
They resemble the shapes of a lighthouse, a web, or even an old pirate ship.
The children pretend they're a ship lost at sea, a lighthouse their only redemption,
Or a fly caught up in the tangling web, trying to distract the spider's attention
Some of them take on the role of a rogue and with cunning their friends they outrank
As pirates they hoist the Jolly Roger on board, and force them to walk the plank
The technology of today is a wonder, it adds new dimension to fun,
But imagination's the key to it all, without it no adventure could run.
It's irrelevant what kind of apparatus is used, or what age the

user has achieved
The key to enjoyment of all ages is the ability to imagine and believe.
The park, it provides a playground for all, where everyone can come to enjoy
The sense of adventure experienced each day by every girl and boy
Mums and dads and grandparents in their own way can join in the fun,
Since imagination's the key to where every single adventure's begun
God has blessed each one of us with the gift of imagination,
From the youngest to the oldest, it's a characteristic in our creation
It can turn a boring object into something of enchantment,
And in our lives can prove a special tool to cause enhancement
And for this special blessing we give our Father greatest praise,
For so many different reasons in our lives our thanks we raise
He fashioned us so carefully and knew each gift we'd need,
And He offers imagination to us, that our fun times can succeed.

The Beach

The grains of sand upon the shore, too numerous to count
Speckled shells and pebbles are found in vast amounts
The waves encroach upon the beach and foam with swirling splendour
They etch the shoreline with great care, the artist, God, their sender
With every careful brush stroke he paints a scenic sight
And people come to wonder and share in His delight
The atmosphere he conjures,is of pleasure and of fun
To relieve our daily stresses to the beach we often come
When the sun in all its glory shines out with radiant ray,
Our minds are turned to surf and sand, on the beach our children play
With buckets and with spades they mould the sand with great precision
A fortress, or a castle with a moat, their chief decision
They prove to be the budding architects of sand and sea
And Mum and Dad stand marvelling at how creative they can be
They splash and swim and in the tide they actively enjoy
A sport, that holds a great appeal to every girl and boy
The beach can also prove to be a place of solitude,
On cooler murky days it's atmosphere a change of mood.
A perfect place to meet with God, to share His company
To open up our hearts to Him, commune in harmony
No greater place than this has God created just for us,
To ease away our tensions and relieve us from life's fuss
And we should go there when we can, it's purpose God has planned,
To be a recreation, meeting place between God and man.

The Spider

One of God's tiniest little creatures, though a genius none the less
How he weaves his wondrous web no human mind could guess.
His supply of threads is endless, he works with tireless effort
No time to take a moment's rest, his work his only comfort
As we watch his spectacle unfold before our eyes,
A wondrous masterpiece he crafts as gravity he defies
Each segment worked with mastery, precision and with care,
This mathematical little genius constructs his form with flair
An articulate piece of tapestry this creature soon displays,
Its nature built to capture his unsuspecting prey
He watches still and silent in his lair of silken weave,
Confident by his effort his hunger will be relieved
To us it may sound cruel, but it's all in God's own plan
The food chain proves a necessity, even in the life of man
On inclement days the spider's web displays its glorious splendour
Encrusted pearls of glistening rain reflect God's love so tender
The sights and signs of nature show proof to living man
That God has fashioned everything, each purpose he has planned
In every living masterpiece, God blessed our world so much,
And man in communion close to nature, with God can keep in touch.

Ireland's Countryside

Ireland is a land of green, its fields a patchwork splendour,
The trees align their borders, stretching heavenward, tall and slender
The bushes, shrubs and hedgerows, caress the landscape, adding texture,
The multi shades of blended green, a most successful mixture
A carefully woven tapestry, crafted by the Master's hand,
No finer work of art in great world galleries can be found
Streams of cool clear water snake across fields here and there,
Trickling pebbled brooks complementing greenery with great flair
The sunrays golden shimmer reflect the rippling pathway glazed
And provide welcome refreshment for the cattle as they graze
The snowy fleece of sheep and lambs provide a dappled surface
And nature's beauty displays that God fashioned his countryside for a purpose
It's not just pleasing to the eye but serves to provide a home,
Where God's farmland beasts over field and dell can safely feed and roam.

Nature's Playground

God's wooded wetland, nature's playground, fronded firs its pathways line
Lakes a mass of webbed-foot wonder plunge and dive, on seed to dine
A mother moorhen shows maternal instinct, as she collects the seed
Pecks it from the water's depth, hungry open-mouthed chicks to feed
The haughty long-necked geese approach, their ravenous greed to satisfy
They hiss and spit their discontent at unsuspecting passers-by
Along the pathways insects hover, through the greenery search out their prey
A dragonfly flits its delight; it's caught a moth along the way
In graceful flight, a butterfly its fragile wingspan flaunts with pride
It flutters amid the foliage, alights a leaf, with poise to hide
Walking through the pathways' rustle, a carpet laid of leaves and cones
Logs are stacked, chopped and hacked, while untidy grass is skilfully mown
Thickets bounce to life, as hopping bunnies dart about their way
Waterfalls gush rushing water, swirling, bubbling, sheer rocks to spray
Owls aloft the tree tops hidden, watchful hoot at passers-by
Bushes crack and pop shrill noise, as seedpods burst their nature's cry
Fluffy newborn ducklings huddle, compete for comfort from

their mates
A whiff of burning pine and timber nature's odorous story relates
Above the leafy arbours tall the dappled sky beams down God's heat
The sight resembling a child's expression, a carefully finger-painted feat
A blessing to the human eyes, the ears, the heart, God's wondrous work
In admiration we share God's glory, on us it leaves an awesome mark
This world He fashioned tenderly, each creature's home He built with pride
And we with God through wooded wetlands marvel His creation, side by side.

God's Ocean

The sea a mirage in the sun, with glistening diamonds inset
With shimmers, ripples sparkle, where their surface sunshine met
Encrusted ocean's splendour, no jewel ever match
God's radiance, mirrored image, on the waves they gently catch
More precious than fine silver, more priceless than pure gold
God's creation and His love those twinkling waves unfold
The ripples lap, their aqueous hush, "Dear child I love you so,"
No other love on earth compares, of this I surely know
Be still a while and stay with me, my purpose to reveal
My friendship, and your trust of me, I dearly wish to seal
This setting's tranquil splendour, a comfort to the mind
A chance for Me as Master, to commune with humankind
Open up your heart to Me, I long to enter there
And all your world's emotions, with you I wish to share
I'll stay with you forever; I'll never from you stray
And we will walk life's sandy shores, forever and a day.

The Old Log Fire

The day is drawing to its close
A time for well-deserved repose
The challenge of the daytime won
Relaxation now to come
Strike up a match, rekindle the flame
The initial lick of fingers tame
The lavish orange ember glow
Embracing logs as flickers grow
Dancing with such flurried flight
Choreographed with sheer delight
The flickering flame an energy source
Provides with atmospheric force
The warmth so tender, pleasant, calm
An airy, pensive, relieving balm
In sure repose outstretched with care
The soothing sway of the rocking chair
Adds to the mood of serenity
The ligneous aroma of tranquillity
The colour change from red to white
Logs ashen disintegrate from sight
With cracking sound and roaring blaze
Heat radiates a smoke-filled haze
With feet reclined and distant minds
Warm atmosphere to help unwind
To stare amid the reddish glow
Imagination and thoughts full flow
Pictures prance amid the red
While kindling keeps the fire well fed
And as it dies its embers bright

Fill the grate with warmth and light
The flame recedes the logs expire
Ashes are all that's left of our fire
A perfect way to end the day
Reclined amid the embers' ray.

Day And Night

Daytime is a blessing, when God turns on His light
His radiant ray beams down in day to illuminate His sights
Some days He turns the brightness low, a duller day to form
He clouds the skies with cotton wool, but keeps us temperate, warm
As rain clouds in the skies appear, the drip from water tap
Showers our flowers and trees, to quench their thirst while sunbeams nap
The dampness sometimes causes an electrical elapse
And lightning crashes to the earth, its noise thuds with a zap
Accompanied by thunder, as the cloud bursts clap their hands
It's all in God's creation, the weather predicted and well planned
And as the day comes to its close, to bed we all retire
God switches out His light to extinguish daytime fire
He hangs the stars up in the dark, to twinkle and to shine
The blackened edge of evening clouds their images refine
His moon appears, its glowing sphere, to cast its shadow there
And all who see its radiance, at its glory stand and stare
And by vision of these wonders who could deny that God's in charge
No human mind could ever fathom this science, it's too large
Please give God all the glory as you study nature's glare
And believe in your heart that, without God, nothing's there
This earth is His creation, the sun, the moon and stars
And he has hung them in the sky by His almighty power.

Earth's Beauty; Heaven's Glory

This tranquil setting, Heaven sent,
Sights and sounds by God are lent
Given to us to appreciate how
God in His heaven his glory can show
It's impossible to dare even comprehend
The experiences heaven to us will lend
But commune with your Father, He'll show through His love
The eternal pleasure awaiting you above
Just close your eyes to hear God speak
His voice through sounds of nature leaks
The rustle of the wind, blown trees
The buzz of very busy bees
The sweetest song that's ever heard
Sweetly performed by tree-perched birds
The river gushing to and fro
Unsure which way to flow
Silence, His music to our ears
While nature assures us that God is here
He whispers, "I love you" in each precious sound
To prove to the world He's everywhere around
And in hearing His voice, we open our eyes
A magnificent picture before us He lies
His awesome creation carefully unfolds
From biblical text, of this often we're told
The sun, the moon and stars by night
They shine and twinkle, His sky to light
The earth, the trees, the colourful flowers
Are proof of His creative powers
The creatures of both water and land

All crafted by God's mighty hand
The glory of each natural form
Bares its own creature's charm
But best of all, His master plan,
On the sixth day God created Man
And every natural sight we see
He created just for you and me
So if you marvel at earthly splendour
Trust in God, their faithful sender
For He has prepared a place for you
Of glory in His skies of blue
His beauty on earth will never compare
To the magnificence in Heaven He's created there
And the sight of our Lord seen face to face
Will be an experience of amazing grace
It's impossible to envisage the sights that we'll see
His splendour is waiting both you and me
So if you've enjoyed all his sights and his sounds
While living on earth where his nature abounds
Just imagine the pleasures awaiting you there
In His great big blue yonder with your Master to share.

Family and Friends

Baptism

Our daughter's such a blessing
 And we give thanks to the Lord
These promises that we make today
 We'll strive to keep our word
We'll raise her with care and affection
 And teach her of God's love
And pray throughout her life
 That from his care she'll never move
And when she comes of age
 To make these promises for herself
We pray that she has spiritually grown
 In mind and soul with health
That she will continue to follow the Lord
 With the love instilled in her heart
And she with her Lord a partnership form
 That will never keep them apart.
 In confirming her faith in her Father above
 Our promises she'll finally fulfil
And trusting her life to him every day
 She'll live to obey his will.

Our Daughter

No words could ever tell
The feelings deep within our hearts
When this tiny little bundle
Her life about to start
Was placed within our caring arms
Surrounded by our love
No words could ever express the joy
God sent us from above

Her name by God already known
She has made our lives complete
From the wrinkles in her button nose
To her wiggly little feet
She smells so sweet and fragrant
Her skin so soft and tender
To cuddle her is a blessing
We thank the Lord, who sent her

He blessed our family far beyond
No gauge could ever measure
God above has sent his love
In a daughter we can treasure.

You Always Put A Smile On My Face

One morning, while in conversation with my youngest son
Concern and constant worry through discussions seemed to run
He voiced some reservation about returning to his school
Examinations close at hand, afraid he'd prove a fool
I tried to reassure him, to ask God for some help
He didn't have to go through all this pressure by himself
For God already knew what for his life He'd carefully planned
He holds our future in the very palm of mighty hands
It didn't really matter what results those tests would bring
As long as to our Father's will we closely try to cling
Work as hard as possible, and try your best my son
For God already has your future worked out, it is done
He turned to me, the worry eased, the tension seemed erased
And whispered, "Thanks, you always put a smile upon my face"
Such wonderful expression, when faced with God's true love
For He will always smile on us, from heaven up above
And if through life, we need some help with any worrying tasks
He'll smile and say, "I'll help my child, you only need to ask!"

Lessons To Be Learnt Though The Life Of A Child

To watch the beauty of children at play
Their innocence and trust of each other relay
The simplicity in all that they do and they say
Their laughter and playfulness resound through each day
The warmth they both radiate, the beam of each smile
Adults should watch and take stock for a while
If their example we could imitate and follow
Our adult lives might not prove so hollow
To acquire simple trust as a child of her friend
Our mature relationships to approve and amend
To go back to basics, our youth to re-seed
More childlike behaviour our adulthood needs
To take time out from our busiest days
Relax and recoil in more playful ways
The stresses of our grown-up lives to relieve
Revert back to childhood, our maturity to reprieve
They say "that grown ups always know best"
But with careful consideration put to the test
From the life of a child there are many lessons to learn
And it's time that as adults to our children we turn
To benefit more from their youthful array
And live more fulfilled to the end of our days.

Childhood's Eyes

Her beauty shines through trusting eyes
That gleam and sparkle as she smiles
Their deepest depth of burnished bronze
A mischievous, fathomless chasm form
With fluttering ebony lashes extended
She cleverly flatters, her own way intended
As her chin in the palms of her hands gently laze
The haze of her gaze in its mind-wandering maze
Her eyes watch a vision from a fantasy beamed
With preoccupied stillness she pensively dreams
Reverting to reality she buzzes with glee
She flits and she flaps like a wild honeybee
If faced with adversity the characteristic change
Distresses her glance with variable range
Perplexed and withdrawn her lids softly sink
With emotional perception gestures compassionate blinks
In sadness or suffering a melancholic strain
Fights to contain tearful droplets of pain
But with laughter and giggles she quickly regains
Her twinkling beauty and happiness retains
She'd light up the darkness with her bright beaming eyes
She makes my heart skip every time that she smiles
Her expressive demeanour dawns through every gaze
Various moods reflect in each passing phase
But my favourite of all her looks cute and tender
Come in the evening with peace and serenity rendered
When tucked up in bed her quilt in a huddle
Her dream world to visit and her teddy to cuddle
This through my eyes a beauty to see.

A reflection of sweetness and tranquil humility
And I praise God above for His expressions of love
Tendered to us through our daughter from above
Each day I watch for her childlike reaction
Which proves a characteristic of remarkable attraction
And how her eyes change to reflect all her thoughts
In dreams and deep sentiments often she's caught
And how as an adult I wish to reflect
Her naivety of manner and simplistic trait
By seeing through her eyes my stresses would flee
What a joy to create an adult with childlike simplicity.

Don't Deny Your Children, The Gift of God's Creation

A world filled by technology, machinery, microchips
Rockets zoom off to the moon, we cruise the world in ships
A computer, commonplace, is used in almost every home
Telephones and TVs pocketed, as all around we roam
Washing machines for dishes, not just for dirty clothes
Children spend days endlessly with Game Boys stuck to their nose
Automobiles, our trusty steed, no cause to go on foot
Express trains whiz their pathways through our countryside, and toot
Our skies are overpowered by the jet planes' engine roar
The air traffic controllers can't cope with many more
A book comes second place to TVs and computer games
Think about this rationally, it really is a shame
TV dinners, microwaves, burger outlets by the score
Our children don't appreciate home-cooked foods anymore
They say a plate without a burger, sauce and lots of chips
In their opinion, commonplace, is really just the pits
Many of our technical wizard new friends
Their expertise is needed, to accomplish newer trends
Especially those concerned in medical fields to aid the ill
Their purpose to achieve better diagnosis future skilled
But when it comes to children, I feel they've lost the plot
So many material things in life, too easy for them got
Parents don't have time to spend, their family second place
Opinionated it may be, this behaviour, their disgrace
Their technical career lives more important none the less

Their children left to cope alone in life, "Oh what a mess!"
They're not taught to appreciate the simpler things in life
Their minds are forced and overpowered by educational strife
Today as parents we must try to re-educate our youth
Help them gain a love for life, from God's love learn some truth
That material wealth won't bring the joy our lives are searching out
We need to experience God's true love, that's what life's all about
God's natural world uncovered, no programme on TV
Could match its wondrous beauty as we gaze in reality
To spend a day along its path, fulfilled by visions given
No computer disk compares, this adventure world it is God driven
With different outlook, they are blessed, amazement on their faces
Their minds awash amid fresh air, their blushing cheeks refreshes
Is technology a better option, or are our lives just simply spoilt?
Suppose before it gets too late, we give ourselves a jolt
Please don't deny your children the gift of God's creation
It opens up their minds and hearts, removes so much frustration
An opportunity for parents to grow closer to their child
A stronger bond, relaxed, enjoyed, technology put to the side
Remember, live your life to the full, there's only one to enjoy
And use each precious moment to share with God your girls and boys.

Your Teddy Bear

Fur so soft, a fluffy nose
Bedtime companion with furry toes
Cuddly, cute, huggable curls
Cosy comfort for boys and girls
Sweetest smile, with tender cheer
Arms outstretched, two soft ears
A trusted friend, of cushioned form
Keeping you from nightmares' harm
Skip through dreamland, safe, secure
Knowing that your guard is there
Your flexible friend with legs and arms
To pose is one of his clever charms
From birth, right up to present age
You feel secure, his face to gaze
A true companion, trusted friend
To keep throughout, to life's journey's end
You whisper secrets in his ear
Only things for him to hear
He holds your secrets in his care
No other soul with them to share
He'll never fail your trust in him
With confidence, your heart to win
A friend for life, through cares and woes
Where ever you travel, he also goes
To stroke his textured velvety hair
Comforts your days, he's your teddy bear

For children this concept works a treat
But with maturity, true life you greet

And teddy can't go everywhere
Except, that people stop and stare
It's time to find a different friend
One on whom, like teddy, to depend
He's already there, and waiting too
In yonder clouds and skies of blue
He is our Lord, our Master, friend
On Him our entire life's journey depend
He offers security and tender touch
We'll come to love Him just as much
In fact, we'll love Him even more
Our hearts, our lives to Him outpour
He'll be our new found trusted friend
To carry with us to life's journey's end
And Teddy will be just a toy
That we once loved as girls and boys
With realisation soon to dawn
That God has been there all along
He's the one who's loved us so
Teddy was just a toy, you know
God was our guard, our friend, our guide
Nothing from Him we needed to hide
He was our truth, our life, our pal
It wasn't our dear little Teddy at all.

God's Mansion In The Sky

"Mummy, where does God come from, does He live up in the sky?"
A question from a tiny child, she always asks "But why?"
"Has He built a great big house up there, does it have lots of rooms?
Is He waiting for some visitors, will they go to see Him soon?
Does He have friends and family, sons and daughters too?
We could maybe be His friends, our family, me and you
Mummy can we go there, to see His house some day?
I wonder if we ask, will He show us all the way?
Will we have to buy a ticket, will we go to Him by train?
I wonder will it take us there, and bring us back again?
I bet He'll have a party, He'll be glad to see us come
He'll welcome us with a great big hug, and show us round His home
I'm sure it's really pretty, with lots of things to do
Mummy, what do you think, would you like to go there too?"
A very special image, in a child's mind, of her Lord
His home a welcome presence, no fear to her affords
Instilled by love and trust for Him, she treats Him as her friend
To visit Him in glory, one day, her life's true end
But she won't need a ticket; it already has been bought
By Jesus' death, upon the cross, her freedom for her sought
She won't need any transport to take her to this place
Jesus will return to earth, and meet her face to face
And as she grows to love her Lord, and serve Him through her life
He'll help her cope with all life brings, the trouble, joy and strife

And when the time has come, her life on earth its flame extinguished
Her human life existence one day will be relinquished
The vision she once dreamed in childhood, will be reality
And in God's heaven and His home, will live for all eternity
He'll welcome her with open arms, to stay close by His side
Forever in His presence, His child with Him abide.

What Is A Mother?

When God sent me down from his heavenly realm,
To be born here on earth, my Birthday
He blessed me for life, from beginning to end,
With a treasure, forever to stay
She comes in a form that is tender and warm,
Her wisdom instructs me each day
She protects and directs as she guides me in growth,
And keeps me from all of harm's way.
In all that I do, she's included too,
Each day as we keep close in touch
Not often enough said, remiss I'm afraid,
That by me she is loved very much
In my joy, in my fun, since my life has begun,
She's the centre of all I employ,
She can join in the race, and keep lively pace,
And her life's effervescent with joy
She's a companion, a mate to whom I relate,
On her I can always depend
I can tell her my all, my confidante call,
But prefer just to call her my friend
If I hurt or I ail, she never will fail
To surround me with caring and love
She reflects and she acts, as a matter of fact,
In the will of our Father above
And as from above, with his care and his love,
He sent her to make me a home
She'll always be there, with her love and her flair,
And I'm proud I can call her, "My Mum!"

Our Parents, Our Best Friends

Many elderly people need to feel God's love today
Behind closed doors we're ignorant how do they live that way
Aged parents left to cope, alone all by themselves
Their children busy living life have left them on the shelf
Debilitated by their years, too frail to get around
And still their offspring don't take time to visit, they are frowned
Able to cope with strangers' needs, no task to them proves large
Yet first, they should consider their poor parents, take full charge
Instead they leave this task to strangers, responsibilities they fail
And yet refuse acceptance that their parents now are frail
An opportunity lost to show their folks how much they care
And often find, that it's too late when they're no longer there
This leaves them with a burden, too hard for them to cope
The realization that their lack of care gives little hope
Of ever gaining back the precious time which they have lost
Their lack of interest in their care, how much this ignorance cost
Our parents are a precious gift God gives us when we're born
With love and cherished feelings our lives for us adorn
They spend a lifetime caring, and moulding as we grow
Their hardships and their sacrifice we'll often never know
And as their years increase, they are less able to cope with life
Their children should be their stronghold, remove all fear and strife
That they may feel secure in us as we did once in them
That we do all they did for us, treat them just the same
To be there every day, relieve their worries and their fears

To love and cherish, give them worth, remove their saddened tears
Bring joy into being, and enjoyment, laughter too
Give them opportunity to be part of life with you
They'll leave this life more dignified, enjoy their family to the end
And we'll have precious memories of our Parents, our Best Friends.

My Husband

Of all the ladies in this world, I know I'm blessed the most
To me God gave the perfect partner, although I should not boast
And from the day he had us meet, up to the very present,
The love that's grown, the feelings shown, have proven very pleasant
The day that we were married, the words we said,"I do",
Forever I'll be thankful that those words I said to YOU!
Our marriage is a blessing, to which God has richly given,
 His love, compassion, tenderness, by Him it's safely driven
Our love we share together, runs deeper than any river,
And richer still because it's shared with God its very giver
We've climbed many mountainous hurdles, yet overcome each one,
But would have failed except by faith in Jesus, God's own Son
We've shared much joy and laughter, some sadness and some tears,
But each emotion felt, we've shared together, throughout the years.
No matter what life throws at us, our bond intact remains,
With God as Guide, I pray this trend will never, ever change
Each day when I awake, I know you are my special friend,
With whom I share my life, and in whom I most definitely depend
You are my sun, my moon, my stars, my nighttime and my day,
The love I feel deep in my heart for you will ever stay
You provide me with protection, you love me at my worst,
In life I know for certain that you always put me first
You're kind and generous in every way, in all you say and do,

A comfort and a trusting friend, a willing partner too
I've penned these words because I love you more than words can say,
Endless pages could never express the feelings I hold every day,
For the love of my life, my companion, my friend, my helper, my comfort, my all,
All my worries, my fears, my troubles, my tears, my elations on you I can fall
For the blessing of you, so precious a gift from the Lord, for the rest of my life,
I will shower Him with praise, and give thanks every day, and be proud that we're HUSBAND AND WIFE!

Age And Youth In Harmony

In a secluded country setting, the old oak tree stands tall
Its branches, arms stretched open wide, to welcome one and all
Its leaves provide protection from stormy winds and rain
Each ray of glistening sunlight reflect their dew kissed grain
Its trunk is aged and wizened, gnarled and textured deep
Its solid base is strong and firm, an anchorage to keep
Each knotted twist of bough and twig stretch wide with form and might
Beginning from the rooted trunk, to stretch both left and right
And from these horizontal beams two man-made swings suspend
Two children gaily playing, on this tree's strength they depend
The sun's rays radiate their smiles, the wind wisps through their hair
They laugh and frolic endlessly, their world without a care
To think that an ancient arbour such fun and joy could lend
Where nature with its strength and children's playfulness now blend
The children reflect their youth and vigour, against the age-old tree
Yet both their characteristic years blend well in harmony
The tree supplies reliable strength, with age it has matured
The simplistic trust the children hold ensures they are secure
And so it is throughout all life, where young and old both blend
Mature of age and youthfulness, on each other can depend
The experience of life's elders offers mentoring to the youth
Their wisdom, knowledge and years of growing, a passing on of truth

Yet from the young, the old can learn to regain their youthful ways
And re-enact the playfulness of their by-gone childhood days
And both can join in union, like the tree and playful child
A relationship secure and strong, in trust they learn to build
They each learn from the other, their strengths and weakness blend
And soon they grow to be through life dependable true friends.

Neighbours

There are many different things in life we often take for granted
And many times we seem to get the things we've always wanted
We're never satisfied, we're always wanting more and more
The material things in life we seem to gather by the score
We waste so much in life, it doesn't even cost a thought
Since food and drink and daily needs are so often easily bought
Yet spare a thought for those around who find life less resourceful
At many of their mealtimes they don't even share a morsel
And many times of loneliness, no friends to share their day
They spend their time in solitude with little words to say
Yet we can oft offend the many friends that we have got
And even as we do it, it doesn't mean a lot
You may not realise that people near you live like this
And struggle every day in life to barely just exist
Be vigilant of those nearby, who live quite close to you
And offer them a listening ear in everything you do
And if a needy person shows that they might need a favour
Then you by acts of selflessness could prove to be their neighbour.

Friends Are Like Sunshine

Friends are like sunshine that brighten our way
With each radiant smile they light up the day
They share in our laughter, they dry up our tears
They remain in close contact through many long years
You can confide in a friend, and know that they're there
To share in your burdens, your joys and your care
You'll never be lonely, you'll never be dull
Cause you know on a close friend you always can call.

One minute of your time is all that it takes
One minute in time all the difference it makes
To make someone's life more easy to bear
To show by your actions that you really do care
So if you know someone who's lonely today
Contact or call them, your friendship display
And some day if you find that you're in need too
They will display the same caring to you.

Friendship

Friendship is a gift from God
To bind us close together
And when he brings two people close
He keeps them there forever

A friend can wipe away a tear
A friend can share a joke
A friend can listen with great care
Not like some other folk

They help each other when in need
They shop until they drop
They baby-sit to let you out
Their talents never stop

Relationships between two friends
That God has brought together
The bond they share will never tear
He'll keep them friends forever.

God's Healing Power

Share The Good News

Amid the busy bustle of the city streets one day
Shoppers queuing, browsing, buying gaily on life's way
A sudden realisation, amid the sea of faces
The multitude of ages and many different races
Consider, have these people ever heard about God's love?
About the Son He sent to live on earth from heaven above
Do they know He cares for them, by grace can change their being?
Add hope, and joy, and purpose, to their lives bring inner meaning
They may be just too busy now, not interested to hear
Or don't have time to go to church, young families to rear
They reason that God's not for them, they'll manage on their own
Or think their lives are not too bad, no harm they've ever done
If they took time for God, He'd not allow them to have fun
With excuses and apologies, from their situations run
Such a sad dilemma, for without God they can't live
They need the love, compassion, joy and freedom that He gives
It's not until God's in the centre, their life around Him built
That He removes all fear and stress, and human ridden guilt
These people shouldn't have to live in ignorance of God's love
There's so many different ways to act, its presence to them prove
We are His instruments; we have His gospel to proclaim
Use your gifts that He has given, today spread wide His name
Instead of allowing sinful addictions to overtake our world
Fling wide the gates of heaven, God's banner now unfurl

We need to share His message, to give these people hope
With knowledge of God's love they have a better chance to cope.

Do Unto Others, As You Would Have Them Do To You

Would you wish your life to be ignored and pushed around?
People stamp all over you, they treat you as the ground
They push their way in front of you, as if you were not there
They always think about themselves, for others share no care
Their jobs are more important, their needs always come first
Their treatment it frustrates you, you see them at their worst
You try to make them realise that you are standing there
But they just look straight through you, through selfish eyes, they stare
Too wrapped up within their world, they just don't notice you
Standing at that lift or waiting for hours in that bus queue
They push you to the side, they're more important, don't you see
What selfish, ignorant, self-centred lives, they seem to live in glee
The world owes them a favour, it's not their fault you know
That every deed their lives project, each day in ignorance grows
And as you watch their actions, you contemplate their lot
And think yourself quite fortunate, their traits you haven't got
But you are so mistaken, because you do the same things too
And now you've sadly realised, these characteristics, not so new
Remember yesterday, that lady standing at the till
Your parking ticket running low, you had to pay your bill
She'll not mind, I'll jump the queue, you whisper to yourself
She'd do the same to me, if found in that position herself
And now you're in those self-same shoes, you've acted just the same

You contemplate a while, and pray, "Oh Lord please help me change"
Help me put others before myself, my selfishness erase
Self-centredness and selfish ways, from my life please quickly chase
Let all who come in contact with me throughout the day
Feel that I have treated them in a very favourable way
That through my thoughtful actions I may keep this motto too
Do only unto others, as you'd have them do to you.

GREED!

Greed is such an awful sin
Encompassing the world we're in
Changing love within man's heart
Pulling many lives apart
Aiming to undo God's work
Just another Devil's quirk
Making man oppose what's right
Selfishness his main delight
Always wanting for himself
Never sharing with his wealth
Spending money needlessly
Unaffected by poverty
Gluttonous when eating food
While others starve, it isn't good
Children starved of love as well
No one in their world to tell
Stop right now, it all must cease!
Our greedy ways we must decrease!
Act right now and look around!
Solutions surely can be found!
Change our selfishness for love
And ask for help from God above
Work as a team, our world will change
The answer isn't all that strange
For God has built our world on love
Which we with greedy hearts disprove
But with our change of heart can save
The lives of those who little have
If we erase our negative form

With kindly deeds our world adorn
And through our actions generously spread
Some worthwhile helpfulness instead
Not just in actions but in word
Reflect the life of our dear Lord
And trust in Him to know what's right
He'll aid us with the will to fight
We'll find we've made a dramatic improvement
A kinder less selfish God-filled environment.

God Knows What Is Best!

If your life is upside down, you don't know were to turn
Problems come from every angle and for comfort you often yearn
If you're going through a stressful time, a very difficult stage
And wish that you could simply turn over a new page
If you feel that just right now you're at the end of your wits
The world that you're accustomed to is slowly falling to bits
Stop a moment, listen, there is great news for you!
God knows exactly how you feel, He went through it too!
So never be discouraged, I know it's hard to do
But no matter what's gone wrong in life, He will take care of you
At times when at our weakest, He carefully builds us up
He knows that deep inside He's made our will of stronger stuff
We don't need vitamins or pills to lift us from our fate
Just trust in God, He'll share our load, it'll never be too late
At times we feel our lives are spinning way out of control
But God is in command, He'll always point us to His goal
We must endure with patience and take comfort from His Word
Don't make rash decisions, simply wait upon Our Lord
And very soon an answer will reveal itself to you
Not necessarily the answer you feel that you are due
But God in all His wisdom, He knows what is best
And if we trust Him with our lives, He'll surely do the rest
It may take years before you reach your final destination
But every twist and turn in life prepares for your vocation
And God uses each experience, no matter bad or good
To shape our lives into the form as only God Himself could
Our lives are clay within the caring articulate potter's hand

And with patience, trust and loving care, will work out as He's planned
So when you hit a rough patch in your life don't be depressed
But know that through your hardship, God your life has surely blessed
And when through time you do reflect on all that you've been through
I'm sure that your decision is, That God's Been Good To You.

Life Is Like A Yo-Yo

Life is like a yo-yo, it has its ups and downs
Depending on who holds the string determines what comes round
If through our own decision we think we know what's best
The result may not be favourable, we may not pass the test
But if at first, before we act, we ask for intervention
Of a loving heavenly Father, who with every good intention
Wishes that in everything all will work for good
And in trusting His decision we will find it should
So let us learn our lesson, that as long as we allow
God to pull the strings in life, He will work out how
The final result in everything becomes a positive one
Because to us He sent the gift of His ever loving Son
And before He ever gave us birth, our lives for us He scanned
And although He gave us freedom to make all our own plans
He hoped that we would use our choice and accept our Lord and Saviour
And in doing this we would certainly be doing ourselves a favour
So before you make decisions, no matter how big or small
Be reassured that God is there to help you with them all
As long as every day you place your cares within His hands
Everything will work for you, as God Himself has planned.

There Is So Much Competition

There is so much competition in our everyday routine
Sometimes it's a good thing, but it can also prove quite mean
Some in life are quite prepared to go the extra mile
But others sometimes jump the queue, then stand and sneer a while
Yet none of this is necessary, as the race has already been won
The victor's name is Jesus Christ, God's very special Son
He died to give new meaning to our everyday lifestyle
And He's the true and only One who went the extra mile
He wants us to commune with Him, our lives to energize
Because in life He surely is the only lasting prize
His team consists of you, the Father, Son and Holy Spirit
And if through life you run the race His way you'll win with merit
It's a very special team He's made, He wants you to take part
In each daily race He'll run with you, but before you even start
You can be sure He has already planned your every movement
And that competition in your life won't add a single improvement
So run the race with keenness, in this special team of four
And you will always close the daily race with a very perfect score.

Slow Down In The Fast Lane

Have you ever felt your stress far too much to bear
Your mind is in a frazzle, and you're pulling out your hair
Daily pressures build on you, your shoulders feel like lead
The weight they carry much too heavy, pains shoot through your head
"Get this finished", "Do that job", "Have you got that done?"
Stress is wearing out your life, you don't have any fun
In your mind's conclusion, this is how life's meant to be
Yet quite the opposite is true, relax, from stress, be free
Your best decisions, works and tasks, succeed more while relaxed
When your mind's at restful peace, you're on more positive tracks
Living in the fast lane, today's society at its best
But we mere mortals don't realise our bodies need more rest
Cholesterol levels soaring, more heart attacks and strokes
This new age of stressful life puts pressure on us folks
This race that we are running, put down the starter's gun,
Slow your pace, you'll win this race by having much more fun
The job will still get finished, take one thing at a time
Those mountains straight in front of you are still too high to climb
And you will find, that when you slow your life right down a pace
The tasks you have before you are far easier to face
In fact you will enjoy them, more focused on their worth
A more creative, positive attitude to each job, given birth
Your productivity increased, accomplish so much more

Tomorrow's challenge, less stress to bring, won't seem such a chore.

(Deuteronomy 33:25) ...and as thy days so shall thy strength be.

Our Province Needs God's Love

Our province needs the love of God to bring about true peace
Unless our hearts are filled by Him, this war will never cease
No bomb or bullet, gun or knife can truly bring contentment
Instead they only offer sheer and bitter hate – resentment
No human reasoning could honestly think – by taking someone's life
That this could prove the answer to our province full of strife
It only acts to accumulate more killings, tit for tat
An unending state, catch-22, is now just where we're at
The pain, the grief, the suffering, the fear already caused
It's time to take a stand and reason out our many flaws
For thirty years, this way of life, of human desecration
Has gone against all laws of God and ruined this our nation
Each time a life is taken, God weeps a million tears
Imagine all those rivers cried, throughout these thirty years
He wants us all to live as neighbours, no fences to divide
To rid ourselves of politics and evil human pride
To live together friend and friend, equal to each other
Sister as to sister and brother as to brother
He loves us as His children, but we often need chastised
To bring us to our senses, to remove our selfish pride
This war has got us no where, we're right back where we started
It's time all human approaches to our situation departed
It's God's time now, so turn to Him, He'll instruct us through each day
Just trust in him and ask for strength, he'll show us all His way
We've learned we're no good on our own, we need Him as our guide
And faithfully through our troubled past, He'll truthfully abide

To Him this country's precious, but its people even more
Our past has been a sacrilege – it's hurt God to the core
So place Him in the centre of our lives, it's not too late
He will wash away our wicked sin, renew and clean the slate
Replace all hatred with God's love, repent of all we've done
And God our country's answer will redeem us by His Son
To refuse this one-time offer, when the end of time has come
You'll have to answer to your Lord for all the things you've done
He won't be lenient with His law, He'll sort you out, my friend
An eternity spent in furious fires is just where you will end
So don't take too long, make your choice, repent before it's too late
Accept God as your Master, His love for you is great
Decide between this war and God, I know which one I'd choose
With God as strength within your life you'll never, ever lose.

Jesus Wants To Care For You

If you're lonely, if you're blue
Jesus wants to care for you
If you want to chat a while,
Conversation's just His style
If you have a joke to tell,
He can laugh at it as well
If you're worried, say a prayer,
He can ease your troubles there
He's the master of all things
Everything to Him now bring
Treat Him as your closest friend
One on whom you can depend
He's there to share each precious moment,
On all aspects of life to comment
He's known you from the very start
And in all your life wants to be part,
To share your sadness, cares and woes
Your laughter, joy and protect you from foes
He wants to enjoy every moment with you
And knows that you'll benefit from His input too
And don't forget His life on earth,
He Himself was given birth
He's already lived throughout a life,
Filled with troubles, with laughter and strife
But He gave everything for you,
To let you experience life anew
So trust Him with your life today,
Get on your knees to Him now pray
And ask Him to forgive your sins,

Open your heart and let Him in
He'll open up a whole new world,
A new dimension to your life unfurl
Trust in Him your whole life through
Your Saviour will always take care of you.

Celebrate God's Love

Celebrate God's love for us; He holds the key to life
No matter if in success we live, or dwell in poverty and strife
A businessman, financially sound, can dwell within God's favour
Yet those less prosperous are his equal, if they know Jesus as their Saviour
In short, it doesn't really matter where we stand on earth
Each of us has a given purpose, which God holds with great worth
As long as we proclaim Him King, that's all that really matters
Because, without the Saviour's saving grace, our life's in tatters
He gives us each a task on earth, our lives already planned
Accept His saving power, it's God's wondrous gift to man
He'll meet us where we stand today, with all our imperfections
To guide us to a better life, renew our self-direction
He wants us to accept His love, we are His chosen ones
God proved this when He sacrificed His very precious Son
But now His Son abides on high and prays for us each day
And when we reach His heavenly home, He'll welcome us to stay.

God's Healing Place For Man

Medical intervention
To cure is its intention
Spotlessly disinfected
Its patients are protected
Compassion, care and love
Staff driven from above
A place of wilful purpose
A much needed service
In the blink of an eye
A newborn baby's cry
In the hush of a ward
Someone's left to meet with God
In pain and in fear
Many patients linger here
Skilful surgeons operate
Their knowledge to deliberate
Trust and dedication
To deal with medication
New concepts and new skills
To cure and ease all ills
Mixed emotions race
The corridors of this place
Birth and death together
Amidst illnesses to weather
To heal and to decide
Our Maker as our guide
A hospital's place
To provide a healing base
With God and Man together

This vocation proves a treasure
Guided by His hand
God's healing place for Man.

The Physician

A devotional profession, God's science, bold and true
A surgeon's hand is guided by God's care, for me and you
The precision and the wisdom required to carry out their work
Such intricate manoeuvres, an unenviable quirk
But, controlled by God's almighty hand, the surgeon never stalls
Trusting in his Master's guidance, for constant help he calls
His knife a dextrous tool of hope, with patience he endures
Many lives depend on him, through his expertise, they're cured
He treats them with compassion, to ease their troubled mind
His actions are of gentlemanly, courteous nature, kind
Responsive to the urgency, yet gentle with his touch
He learns this tender behaviour from his Lord, who teaches much
A vast responsibility lies before him every day
To carry out his charge he calls upon his Lord to pray
Difficult his decisions, distracting many jobs
Reassured that, by God's grace, no human life he'll rob
His mind must stay alert, a trusting faith, in God believe
And guided by the Almighty Physician, many ailing lives relieve.

Take Time To Be With God, He'll Ease Your Stressful Load

Today's lifestyle is full of stresses
With each hurried action our life distresses
It's time to slow, add new perspective
Place on our lives a new directive
Have you ever taken the time to lie
On a rug in a field, and stare at the sky?
The picturesque ceiling above us exposes
Its cotton wool clouds as they exchange different poses
At first glance, a sea, waves swirling the tide
A wind softly blows, and those tidal waves hide
With a blink of an eye an elephant appears
Sporting long curling trunk and protruding flap ears
A poodle well clipped, presented for Crufts
Those clouds perfectly form, to model its fluff
A galleon of white is a pleasureful sight
As it ferries its cargo through flecks of bright light
A 3D candyfloss forms in great haste
Making mouths water with imaginary taste
A fluffy white bunny thinks Easter is near
As he hops through the sky, to soon disappear
A blossom of images, imaginary to see
Appearing so different, to both you and me
These imaginary sights appeal to the eye
As we focus our thoughts on God's overhead sky
A time to relax, to ponder our minds
To count just how many of these images we find
To marvel the ceiling of God's wonderful world

Hand crafted and textured, for mankind unfurled
Removal of tension and stressfulness ease
Our world-wearied mind to refresh and appease
A moment to marvel, commune with our Lord
Such precious time, He deserves us afford
To thank Him for all in our lives that He's given
And open our hearts to His love, straight from heaven
And given time out, to reflect and unwind
To recharge our batteries, and relax our mind
We can add new dimension to the lives which we live
If some quality time to our Lord we can give
To spend with Him there, while our thoughts He renews
Our bodies refresh and our hearts fill with truth
A refreshed inner peace, and a purpose for life
To gain knowledge of His will, for this we must strive
And while in deep reflection we lift up our eyes
Our Lord fills our hearts with His love, strong and wise
This time in His presence, encompassed by hope
Through this time we spend with Him, by His strength we will cope.

Your Master, Your Lord

Thirst for God, He'll quench your fire
Hunger for Him, His will to desire
Seek His presence in all that you see
Closer to walk hand in hand, there He'll be
Praise Him in all that you do and you say
His loving example to others relay
Listen, His whisper is telling you now
How much that He loves you and wants to show how
He blesses your life every day of the week
His spirit to guide with a conscience so meek
Trust in your Lord He's the best friend to have
His life on a cross He so generously gave
Repay Him with faithfulness, trust in His word
He's your Master, your Saviour, your Friend and your Lord.

God's Love For Man

God Shows His Love

God above showed His love, in a stable cold and bare
He sent His precious Son to earth, to dwell among us there
Mary His mother gave Him birth with Joseph standing by
The angels were in attendance, and told the shepherds why
They had to journey far to find the Saviour wrapped in hay
And this will be to all mankind known as Christmas Day
The wise men brought Him gifts of gold, frankincense and myrrh
The vision it was a sight to see, as they all marvelled there
A star it shone to light the sky for everyone to see
That God had sent His precious Son, to be born for you and me.

The Trinity

God the Father, Son and Spirit, they are different, yet the same
Confusing though it is, it's not just in their names
The Father, He's creator of the Universe and Earth
Yet He is a part of everything, knowing our sadness and our mirth
He was born a little baby, fully God and fully man
And lived on earth among us, a part of His own plan
Jesus came to bridge the gap between ourselves and God
The sacrifice He made for us makes us overawed
When He returned to heaven, the Holy Spirit He did send
Who lives in each believer's heart, our conscience and our friend
And if we wish to walk with God, the Spirit, He will guide
Our path, and also give us power to get through life's high tide
So take the plunge, and ask the Lord to come into your heart
And then you will discover, that you've had a missing part.

Unconditional Love

God's love is unconditional, there's nothing we can do
No earning or no purchase price, its cost is free to you
We're told that nothing's free in life, in fact we're very wrong
Material worth may always cost, but God's love's free to all
No greater gift He's given, no better prize we've won
The work, the cost, the suffering paid by Jesus, God's own Son
He gave His life upon a cross, He suffered and He died
But all He gave, to win our souls, redeemed and justified
Please don't deny your Saviour, think of what He's done for you
It's more than any of your well-known friends could ever do
Don't turn your back upon Him, please meet Him face to face
And you'll be overwhelmed by the warmth of His embrace
He promises to walk beside you every step throughout your day
When perplexities and troubles come, He'll carry you all the way
He'll never leave your presence, He's with you to life's end
Accept the love of God above, repent, your life He'll mend
Open up your heart to Him, and He will enter in
He'll wash away your wrongs in life, however big your sin
He'll change your life forever, more fulfilment to bestow
The plans He has already for your life you'll never know
Unless you accept what He has done, and on your Lord depend
Then you'll have gained life's true companion and Very Closest Friend.

When Trials And Temptations Come

Jesus knows the trials, that we can be put through,
For when He dwelt on earth He suffered and was tempted too
The Devil met Him on a mount, and put Him to the test
But Jesus knew just what to do; God's ways were best
For each temptation offered, He revealed God's holy word
So that from His Father's mission He would never be deterred
He mourned the death of Lazarus, real tears His eyes did cry,
But still He turned to God in prayer; He'd know the reason why
And God rose up His friend from death, to make the folk believe
That Jesus, His own Son, was sent and Him they should receive
And when they nailed Him to the cross the pain His body bore
The nails they pierced into His hand, excruciatingly sore
The crown of thorns pressed on His brow, it pricked until He bled
A spear was thrust into His side, the mocking words they said
But at the last the victor, Jesus overcame it all
And ever is available if on Him we need to call
His suffering in comparison to the trials that we bear,
Seems totally incomparable, yet still in ours He shares
Which proves how much He loves us, and will remain until the end
Our everlasting Saviour, and our dependable true friend
So remember when you're worried, or your life is full of woe
Consider what our Lord went through because He loved us so
And be thankful that He died for us to take away our sin,
Please open up your hearts to Him, He'll gladly enter in
And all the trouble in His life, His trials and His pain
Will never be repeated, He, Our Saviour, is our gain.

Jesus Our Example

Self-gratification
A trait throughout our nation
Looking out for number one
Selfish ways are how life's run
Egotistical, mean and narrow
Unconcerned by causing sorrow
Pre-occupied by self alone
No thought or conscience to atone
A change of heart is sadly absent
We require God's guidance to make us decent
We need our selfish ways to trample
Make Jesus Christ our true example
He self-sacrificed everything
A hope for us in life to bring
Was always putting others first
Even while on the cross they cursed
Helped all those who were in need
Five thousand with little food did feed
Offered compassion to the bereaved
As in their tormented tears they grieved
Healed the sick, the blind, the lame
All to Jesus quickly came
He never spared a selfish thought
His love to others always brought
He died, to give us grace to live
We our lives to Him should give
All these characteristic ways
He still performs in our lives today
Stop our selfish actions now

On our knees to Jesus bow
Ask Him to forgive our sin
Allow His love and kindness in
Give Him thanks for what He's done
Be assured your heart He's won
Open life's new chapter now
His guidance alone can show us how
Our selfish ways soon will cease
His love and compassion to care released
Share your lot, it's much more fun
A new dimension of existence run
By sharing love you'll gain more pleasure
And God will bless you beyond all measure.

Our Special Friend

I'd like to introduce you to a special friend of mine
He's caring and compassionate, and generously kind
He gave His life for me one day, on Calvary He was nailed
Throughout His life His Father's will He never once did fail
He came to earth this very special purpose to fulfil
And though He knew before He came, on earth He would be killed
He never once refused, He carried out as God had planned
And suffered on the cross to redeem us sinful men
My life since I have met Him has been joyful and secure
No matter what life throws at me, I know He's always there
He never lets me down, I can rely on Him each day
And when I want to talk, or confide in Him, I pray
Although I cannot see Him, He's present, ever near
This friend to me remains real close, I hold Him very dear
He feels the very same for me, I know, by faith it's true
That's why God sent Him to the earth these tender tasks to do
I hope this introduction will attract you to my friend
That possibly, you'll meet with Him, and your life He'll amend
That you may come to love Him, the same way that I do
Because everything He did for me, He also did for YOU!

God's Gift Of Senses

Walk with God His hand to hold
In his loving arms He'll you enfold
Listen to His tender words
The sweetest voice you've ever heard
Read the gospel, God's own book
Search its pages for guidance look
Smell the fragrance in nature's flowers
Proof of the almighty creator's powers
Taste and see what God has done
To win your heart by His own Son
And by His will you are alive
Through life, His love will safely guide

To make our existence more to enjoy
God to our bodies, five senses employed
So use these blessed senses throughout your day
To add a more varied, enjoyable ray
These senses bring sunshine as part of their zest
Put each one of them straight to the test
Don't be ignorant of what they can do
Use them to enrich others in your life too
Consider your surroundings with greater intention
And treat those around you with much more affection

To hold a baby, friend or child
Your sense of touch to be fulfilled
To listen to a friend with care
Turn your ear, assure them you're there
To see the source of others' needs

Their lacks and needs to share, no greed
To smell the aroma of nature's earth
And teach your children its value and worth
Taste new friendship, share God's love
Introduce hearts to God above
Never lack, your senses use
A more fulfilling life to choose
And thank your Father God as well
For sight, sound, touch, taste and smell.

Inner Beauty

Beauty on the outside projects from deep within
Even if you are blessed with a pointed nose, or double chin
Beauty is only skin deep, what matters is the heart
A relationship with God is where your beauty has to start
Don't be obsessed with mirrors, or the reflection that you see
If God is on the inside, what beauty there will be
He makes us in His image, no one can deny
That any amount of beauty treatment could ever even try
To match the glory of the Lord, His beauty is unique
And in His image every day to live, is what we seek
If you're lacking confidence about yourself today
Speak and tell Him how you feel, to do this simply pray
He'll change your concept of yourself, instil a more positive view
And slowly you will change your thoughts to a confident, more positive you.
He doesn't want to see you cry, He wants to make you strong
And with His positive vision, He will prove your thoughts were wrong
Don't be discouraged by nasty words, or be hurt by human actions
In God's glorious eyes, you are His bride, you are His beauty attraction
He's already planned, your suitor's at hand, you may not have met Him just yet
But worship your Father, his beauty to gather, and in His time, your partner you'll have met.

Your Love, New Life

Lord, such emotion You have tendered, my life renewed with worth
By saving me, Your precious child, You've given me new birth
A reason now to live my life, proclaim Your love, so bold
And through life's journey, Your spirit assures, my hand You'll safely hold
My heart explodes with joy, Your love for me to comprehend
But the human mind, by trust and faith can only understand
Your wisdom and Your guidance help me walk life's pathways long
With You inside my heart, my every purpose fills with song
To share this love with others, that they may gain the same
And come to trust You as their Saviour, praise Your Holy name
Please through my life reflect Your love, let me show how much You care
And through every deed I do, may I know Your love for all I share.

You Are God's Original

You are God's original, there's no one quite like you
He's fashioned and He's formed you, as no other One could do
He has a perfect plan for you, set before the world began
He holds the blue print firmly in the palms of mighty hands
He knows for where you're destined, each step in life you'll take
And each and every footprint with you He'll carefully make
He'll be your strength in weakness, His comfort He'll bestow
Upon you, when your ebb drops down He'll raise you back to flow
He'll smile when you experience the joy He has to give
And weep with deep compassion, when through sorrows have to live
He'll join with you in laughter, He likes to share your fun
And ease your quickened footstep, when through stressful times you run
No one else on earth can carry out your life, but you
And He will guide your purpose, add success to all you do
You are His precious child, He cares much more than you'll ever know
And with grace has provided you original worth, because He loves you so.

God's Purpose

Walk along life's pathway, your Saviour by your side
Never from His will to stumble, from His face to never hide
For you He has true purpose, He's waiting for your call
He'll outpour many blessings, His favour on you fall
Be still a while and listen to the whisper in your ear
His Spirit is your conscience, He'll make God's message clear
He'll guide you with compassion, show you what to do
He knows each step along the way, He'll take good care of you
Confused and strange you'll often feel, His hands, your life will mould
Trust His might and wisdom, God's true purpose will unfold
Don't concern yourself or worry, you're in the Master's hands
And everything within His will, you'll undertake as planned.

The Potter's Hand

We are but a lump of clay, within the potter's hand
To mould and shape, manipulate, His purpose for us planned
 Our Father knows what's best for us, our lives, His death has freed
His will we need to follow, from His Spirit's truth to feed
His touch is soft and gentle, He caresses as He moulds
He fashions every intricate detail, our true form to unfold
With care and concentration, He smoothes our imperfections
Allowing us, His loved ones, to follow His direction
With patience and devotion, He gazes lovingly at His craft
An endless concentrated effort, a multitude of graft
Each tiny change, a closer mark, His perfect image to acquire
He holds our blueprint in His hands, our beauty He inspires
Our lives through torments, trials and temptations, He carefully brings
Reshaping us through passing years, to our final form He clings
Gently folding, pressing, moulding each defect to destroy
A constant change of seasons, our commitment, to Him employs
And as a butterfly through many changing phases comes to be
From egg to caterpillar, chrysalis, then butterfly, fancy free
The cycle of a butterfly, works hard, life's purpose to succeed
As it bursts to wing in graceful flight, from its cocoon, its task, be freed
Our moulding bears resemblance; we change through many phases
With God as guide, our minds, our understanding, He surpasses
And when the final glaze He paints, upon our perfect form
By His grace, we've weathered every season, every troubled

storm
He'll be our force, to push us through, cocooned from worldly strife
And we will soar and spread our wings, His Masterpiece, Our Life.

Friends From Distant Shores

As evening's curtains draw a close upon a perfect day
With sleepy eyes, and tiring mind, sweet slumber dawns your way
The comfort, relaxation, awaiting you within your bed
A fluffy feather pillow to gently rest your weary head
Its warmth and comfort ease the pressures of the passing day
To curl up in its cosy snug, wash tiredness fast away
Succumb to soothing slumber, your mind adrift sleep's sea
What pleasure soon awaits you, in your dreamland, fancy free?
To meet with friends on distant shores, rekindle friendship's touch
To linger there, their comfort share, those companions you loved so much
Watch a while, their radiant smiles with joy fills deep your heart
Then softly slip away, this pleasant meeting to depart
Awake refreshed, your memories last of conversations had
Your mind awhirl, so filled with hope, this meeting's made you glad
And through the day, you carry snippets from this precious talk
And reminisce the visions of where your friends now safely walk
You thank the Lord for restful sleep, that He your night's repose
Has carried you with tender care, while your eyes were safely closed
And some day in another dream, you'll meet Him face to face
Never to wake from slumber, but be received by God's pure

grace
Your dream world now reality, at heaven's gates you'll stare
And all those friends from distant shores will embrace your presence there.

To Meet With Friends Departed

In a quiet country churchyard we pay respects for those departed
Their lives on earth now ended, that which birth for them had started
Each individual life existed, original through and through
A patchwork etched with memories for all those friends they knew
The earth, their comfort's resting place, just for a little while
Until Our Lord returns to earth, to raise them with His smile
He experienced death on earth, but His grave's an empty tomb
He overpowered death's sting, removed its overshadowed gloom
Praise God, He conquered death for us, our life's a passing phase
New hope, receive Him here on earth, into heaven's glory He'll raise
No fear of death He leaves us, we're safe within His arms
Throughout our passing, He will be our guard, our shield from harm
Gazing upon His wondrous face, the dead He'll raise to grace
He'll take them to their room prepared in His wondrous heavenly place
The time between their passing, and His glorious return to earth
Will appear to them a twinkling, just a moment in timescale's worth
Then all other faithful servants, He will raise their lives to share
With those friends, our dear departed, and again their smiles we'll stare.

Accept God's Love

Jesus' love is plain to see, He died upon a cross
He stretched His arms out open wide, and gave His life for us
He asks us to accept His love, it's free to one and all
No payment, it is guaranteed, if on His name we call
He doesn't promise to rid our lives from tension, worry or fear
But through each troubled patch, He'll walk beside us, stay right here
It won't always be an easy task, to live our lives for God
Trust in Him our burden lean, He'll be our strengthening rod
We'll still have many trials and temptations pass our way
His promise is to be our truth; He'll guide us through each day
Don't live within a wilderness, call out to God above
And He will re-direct our lives and show to us His love
We are His children; He cares for us, return His love today
And through life's paths, His righteousness will guide us all the way.

Who Could Ever Deny God?

Who could ever deny there is a God in heaven above?
Who could ever deny, that He surrounds us with His love?
Look around and you will see, the wonders He has made
The landscape He has painted, it will never fade
In every leafy arbour, in every blossoming flower
The wonders all around us prove that He's in power
The birth of a newborn baby and the form that He has moulded
The waves upon a pebbled shore, with precision they are folded
The creatures and the feathered fowl, so many different species
A jigsaw He has carefully crafted, in so many different pieces
He has put them all together and blessed us with His world,
His glorious masterpiece, all around us He's unfurled
But this was just the beginning of His very special plan
He had a perfect reason for the creation of man
It is that all mankind, our hearts they could be won
And so He sent His special prize, His loving, precious Son
To show how much He loves us, He suffered and He died,
And if we put our trust in Him, we are justified
He has washed away our sins and cleansed us from all blame
If we give our lives to Him, we'll never be the same
So don't deny your Lord above, don't waste your life away
Open up your heart to Him and give your life today.

Jesus Your Rock Your Hiding Place

Jesus is our rock, on which to build our hiding place
His stronghold is our refuge, if we seek Him face to face
Through storms and dangers, tragedies, He'll guide us by His hand
With compassion and true kindness, His will to understand
He'll ease our troubled brow, He'll wipe the tearstains from our eyes
His knowledge of the future, structures where our presence lies
We need to show true faith in Him, to trust Him and obey
Our lives a journey, close with Him beside us all the way
In life we'll travel pathways we don't really comprehend
But, He assures that on our journey, we're accompanied by a friend
We may not feel He's leading us in quite the right direction
But He assures, He knows the route, don't face Him with rejection
He's mighty and He's wonderful, a companion warm and true
In times of doubt or trouble, He'll secure all that you do
He is your rock, your hiding place, your stronghold to life's end
A guiding and a trusting Lord, but most of all A Friend.

Don't Shut God Out

Never try to keep secrets from your Father above
Just remember that you are His child, whom He loves
If you're harbouring guilt or burdened with sin
Confide in Him now, run straight up to Him
He'll welcome you gladly with arms open wide
Trust in His tenderness you've nothing to hide
Don't be in fear of Him, don't cause alarm
He will make sure that you come to no harm
Bring all your problems to leave at His feet
With caring and nurture He'll your conscience delete
Have faith in your Lord, He'll know what is best
As long as you trust in Him, He'll do the rest
You'll have the assurance that from you He won't stray
He'll walk close beside you, each minute of your day
As long as you never to Him tell a lie
The bond between both of you never deny
He'll care with compassion, His heart never riled
For He is your Father and you are His child.

Jesus His Purpose To Fulfil

Jesus chose the nails to show His love for all mankind
He didn't have to do it; He could have easily changed His mind
Why did He not request that God remove this daunting task?
The responsibility placed on Him seemed far too much to ask
But He knew He had to face His death, God's purpose to fulfil
And even as He suffered, determined to do His Father's will
The cruel nails, the crown of thorns, the spear gouged in His side
He knew this was His life's true purpose, from this He could not hide
He endured His pain and suffering, He died upon the tree
And all this agony He bore to save both you and me
He whispered, "It is finished" with His final gasp of breath
And gave His body up to conquer over human death
His Father's work completed, a total sacrifice
A one time only mission, never to accomplish twice
The temple curtain torn in two, it was the Father's will
His precious Son redeemed our sins upon that lonely hill
His broken body placed within a borrowed narrow tomb
Clothed in burial array, amid the darkened gloom
A stone rolled over the entrance kept His form away from sight
Only to remain within its grasp, two days and nights
The morning dawned with splendour, an awesome sight that day
The guarded tomb was open, shrouded where the body lay
God had raised His Son to life, oh death where is your sting?
Vanquished, beaten, overpowered, no more its fear to bring
Hope has dawned; the sin of man, by Jesus' death was paid
A ransom, justified by grace, before our hearts He's laid

We only need accept Him, no cost our lives to bring
Acknowledge Jesus as your Lord, the mighty King of Kings
And each year be reminded, in a very special way
That Jesus died and rose for us on that precious Easter Day.

God's Presence Through Life's Storms

God carries us along life's stream, its beauty to expose
Through tranquil daytime settings He gives us sure repose
He whispers through all nature's noise, He says "I love you so"
And echoes this until life's end, no matter where we go
When splashes, swirls and rushing rapids take our lives by storm
Our master's always there at hand, that's when his love proves strong
He'll shield you from the dangers, and keep you from all harm
From winds and waves He'll always keep you safe secure and warm
He'll be the rock to stand on, your firm foundation too
And from the troubles life deflects, He'll take good care of you
Whisper a prayer throughout your day, and keep Him by your side
With God as strength and refuge, with less fear you will abide.

The Rainbow

The rainbow's glory fills the skies
On fluffy clouds God's promise lies
An arc of seven colours blend
No pot of gold found either end
It's there to remind all living things
No fear of flood God's promise brings
A story told of long ago
From bible times, I'm sure you'll know
God told Noah to build a boat
On flooded land he'd safely float
To take his wife and family
Three strong sons, their wives and he
When built he had to fill the Ark
His neighbours thought this was a lark
They laughed and jeered, made so much fun
Unaware of events to come
God sent him animals two by two
To recreate, their task to do
When all aboard God closed the door
For forty days and nights it poured
The evil folk upon the land
All lost their lives, as God had planned
To rid the world of sin and greed
This drastic measure was of great need
Noah's family were saved this fate
Because their love for God was great
They lived their lives within His will
God's decision them not to kill
And when the water's flow had drained

God ceased the skies from pouring rain
Then Noah sent a dove to flight
To ascertain dry land in sight
The dove returned an olive leaf
This to Noah, such relief
Ark rested on a mountaintop
Its floating days to finally stop
And God unsealed the vessel there
All disembarked in His great care
A new world's sight, their eyes to see
This world from evil sin is free
And Noah praised our God above
For showing his family so much love
The evil ways were now destroyed
Loving compassion can now be enjoyed
Much work ahead, for all to do
But God was there to help them too
God gave a sign to Noah high
That flew across the bright blue sky
A glorious reminder, God's promise to show
His precious world, never again He'll o'erflow
And when on a sunny day, clouds in the sky
You catch sight of a rainbow as it passes by
Remember this story, thank God for His care
And know, as with Noah, He will always be there.

God's Miracles, Yesterday, Today and Forever

The winds and waves obey His voice, by Him the sea made calm
He is the shepherd of the sheep, we are His precious lambs
He changed the water into wine, to quench the wedding feast
And on the Mount of Olives true wisdom He unleashed
He fed five thousand folk, with just five fish and two bread rolls
The crumbs left over filled a dozen baskets, twined and wove
He healed the sick, He touched the blind, the lame He made to walk
The people of His time, so much about Him stopped to talk
And it must be the same today, His miracles be told
And to His wondrous presence we must cling and safely hold
And just because to human eye His presence can't be seen
Don't be fooled, He stands right here beside us, on Him lean
In fact His arms surround us each step through life we take
And He for us works miracles, today for His name's sake
With wisdom He instructs our way, His scriptures keep us fed
He heals our ailing bodies, doctors by Him skilfully led
We must proclaim His gospel, today for all to learn
That Jesus Christ is here to stay, to Him we all must turn
We are His precious lambs, He wants to keep us in His care
And He assures us by His spirit, that He is always there
He's not some by-gone character from two thousand years before
He's present in our world today, His children He adores
And in the future He'll come back, we know not time or day
And when He comes, He'll take His trusting servants all away
To live with Him forever, in His heavenly home prepared

And we will live in glory, with our loving Saviour there
And thus fulfil our Father's plan, through time and scriptures too
God, yesterday, today and forever He loves and cares for you.

Speaking With God

Commune With God In Prayer!

Every day as we awake
A few precious moments we should take
To say, "good morning" to our Father above
Thank Him for filling His new day with love
To ask Him, "Lord what shall we do with your day?"
Then wait for His answer as we silently pray
And as we continue, secure in His care
We're assured through this day that He'll always be there
To share in our laughter, our worry, our fear
Should we be sad, He will wipe away tears
He'll listen with intent, as a Father to His child
His ears always open, as we chat for a while
He wants to commune with us throughout each day
And how do we do this – we simply pray
We don't need to use any difficult tongue
He knows all our needs, as before Him we come
So make it a point to keep contact with God
Throughout your whole day He will share in your load
And if every day you continue this trend
You'll find that you've made in Him an everlasting friend.

God's Precious Gift Of Life

Every day when we awake and open up our eyes,
Thank our Heavenly Father; He's given such a prize
Another new day dawning, another chance to live
A gift that only He as Master, God to us can give
He breathes life into each new day, new challenges to bring
He's master of the universe, the earth, each living thing
It's only by His grace we breathe to live another day
And so in great humility our thanks we need to say
Before we race off into daily challenge and routine,
Stop and praise our Father God, we owe Him everything
Ask Him what direction we should take with His new day,
And constantly throughout it ask His will in every way
We need to give our Lord His rightful place in all we do
And trust that in our sharing, by His grace He'll bless us too
He must remain life's centre, His will we must obey,
And He has promised He will walk beside us all the way
Without the air He breathes in us our lives would not exist
And all our earthly opportunities be surely missed
So put into perspective, our dependence takes a twist
God is the sole provider of our life His daily gift
Don't take your Lord for granted, He alone provides the power
To let you keep your life or take it, you'll never know the hour
He's planned your life before He even gave you human form,
And knows each step you'll take, He'll never let you come to harm
Be faithful and prepare for Him, be ready when He comes,
And He will gladly welcome you into His Heavenly Home.

Praise God

Praise God in the morning, He has given this new day
Praise Him then at tea break, some rest He's brought your way
Praise Him in the afternoon, He's helped you through your work
Praise Him that it's teatime in the kitchen while you cook
Praise Him in the evening, as you enjoy good company
Praise Him as you play with kids or chat to family
And as at night to bed retire, praise God for restful sleep
In the knowledge when tomorrow comes, you again He'll safely keep
Throughout your day, work, rest and play, your Lord wants to be part
So hold His hand, He'll guide you and He'll live within your heart
He deserves to be praised all the time, throughout your busy way
So give your Lord His proper place, and praise His name today.

My Life Your Will

Each morning as I wake, Lord, to greet your new-formed day
You whisper poetic lines within my ear and simply say
Put this down on paper, I have a task for you
It is a very special one, I ask for you to do
I want to give you messages, which people need to read
And from those simple lines you pen, their thoughts I wish to feed
To bring them closer to their Lord, through words I give to you
And in their composition, that from me you learn much too
I want to show my endless love, to each and every one
And teach them why I sent to earth my very precious Son
That they may come to love me, and accept His deed for them
He gave His life that they can live, on His risen life depend
Also through these words, instil a very special need
To treat each neighbour as a friend, with true love, from me to feed
That more compassion, kindness and caring nature shared
Spreads throughout mankind, to show, how much for them, I care
A caring human nature can be destroyed by self-esteem
No thoughts for others' needs or cares, it manages to deem
So love your neighbour as yourself, this commandment each to keep
A benefit to all mankind, true love to surely reap
Also through these simple messages, incite realisation to grow
As in their minds, a conscience and a need to change, bestows.

In humility I answer God, please use me for your will
My mind is overwhelmed, and my heart with joy you fill

Remove all thoughts of mine, let these words be only yours
That from their composition, your true love outwardly pours
I know dear Lord for each of us you have a precious will
If this be what is meant for me, I'll humbly it fulfil
To carry out this task will be an honour and a joy
I ask that you will guide me in my path, it to employ
And this is an example how your Lord can ask of you
To carry out His tasks within your life, His will to do
It may not be to write, but to teach or use your gifts
His wisdom will instruct you as your purpose, now you sift
And when you feel He's guiding you please follow where He leads
And he will open every door to place you where He needs.

Using God's Precious Gifts

Lord take my life and use it, as you would have it be
Take everything away from it, that comes from only me
The gifts you've given graciously, please put them to the test
And guide me how to use them, as you alone know best
I yearn to share the love you give with every living thing
Your joy, Your power, Your loveliness to everybody bring
Please guide me through my actions, my deeds, my every word
Allow me to proclaim Your love, my Saviour and my Lord
Without you I am nothing, my life an empty mass
And others in this world without a knowledge of you pass
Please use me as your instrument to direct them in your way
That they may come to learn of you through what I do and say
I don't want recognition or adoration for this task
I only pray that I will carry out all that you ask
That all the praise and glory revert straight back to you
And others see through this my life, what You for them can do
I want to use the gifts you gave, so precious, to full scale
To extend your kingdom, offer hope to others – make God Real.

Fruits Of The Spirit

Lord, you've provided the fruits of the spirit
Through us please use them to show others your merit
Teach us to love as you have loved us
Help us show kindness without any fuss
Let us share joy every day of the week
And let us show faithfulness in relationships we seek
Let us show gentleness and goodness to our neighbour
And make self-control our main daily behaviour
Give us a sense of peace in our mind
That we can serve you through helping mankind
And let us show patience to all in our care
Especially to our children help us to be fair
In all of these attributes, you've given us nine
And in the life of your Son You've supplied us a sign
Of how in our lives you would like us to act
And in your Son's death you've provided the fact
That your love for mankind is so gracious and true
And we owe everything we are solely to you.

Lord Help Us To Show Your Love

Open our minds to your will every day
Teach us to walk along your chosen way
Open our hearts to your love and your care
Help us be kind, and with others to share
Instil peace within us to calm all our fears
Your tender compassion to show through the years
Help us be mindful to others in need
To share our possessions, and harbour no greed
Teach us to speak of your love every day
Reflect You in our lives, some others to sway
That they too will love you, your will to obey
And accept that you'll guide them by trust through life's way.

Let Me Hear Your Voice Lord

Let me hear your voice, Lord
In the stillness of the hour
Let me feel your presence
You are never very far
Let me know your will for me
To trust you and obey
Let me seek your face, Dear Lord
As I kneel down to pray
You gave up everything for me
You suffered and you died
And now my life I give to you
Adored and Glorified.

Today I Lost A Friend Lord

Today I lost a friend, Lord
My heart it ached with pain
But I know I can be happy
For one day we'll meet again
You took her hand and led her home
Her pain she feels no more
And now she dwells with you above
With the Saviour she adored.

Heal The Pain

Lord, I ask for all who weep
That you would dry their tears
Lord, I ask for all who worry
That you would calm their fears
Lord, I ask for all who ache
That you would ease their pain
Lord, I ask for those in trouble
Refresh them in peace again
In you we have such a comfort
In you we have such a friend
In you we have such a healer
On you we can always depend.

Open Up Our Hearts

Open up our hearts, Dear Lord
That you can dwell therein
Make us obedient to your call
And steer away from sin
Guide us with your heavenly hand
And help us show the way
That others may come to love you too
And give their hearts today.

I Know You Are Always There

Lord, when I'm in trouble
I come to you in prayer
I know you'll always hear me
And listen with great care
No matter the size of the problem
No matter the burden I bear
I know that your arms will surround me
I know that you'll always be there.

Telecommunication (Not)

It's just as well that when we need to get in touch with God
A telephone or mobile would never do the job
If this were the only means for God and man to communicate
A conversation between us both we never would relate
Since we with busy lifestyles would never take the time
To have a worthwhile chat because someone else is on the line
And if God wished to contact us, He'd always be enraged
Because every time He dialled the code our line would be engaged
And so God gave a special way to always keep in touch
His ears are ever open, we could never talk too much
We'll never hear a busy tone, no one can tap the line
God will be available to us every single time
It's a direct line up to heaven and no matter what we say
We can talk with God above through every single day
No one can distract us or keep us from the task
If we need to talk with God, we just have to ask
The technology will never break down, no mechanics does it bear
The line is always open and God listens, intent with care
The only fallible part of our two-way conversation
Would be our lack to keep the open line communication
So remember that in everything our Father wants a part
So let Him join each day with you, please open up your heart
Converse with Him throughout each waking moment of your day
You ask, "How do I do this" and He answers "Simply Pray!"

Lord Lead Us By Your Guiding Hand

Lord, lead us by your guiding hand, teach us which way to go
Help us to follow in your will, your love to others show
Make us your instruments, daily used, to bring about revival
That others through our example turn to you for their survival
Give us grace to come to you for everything we need
And from your word of scripture our appetite to feed
Teach us wisdom to know what's right, in everything we do
That we through all our actions render praise straight back to you
Instil in all our hearts an understanding of your book
That we may read through every page, to it for guidance look
God make us patient, kind and true, when others need our care
Help us make them feel secure and reassure them there
When they lack material wealth, please make us generous too
Because the only real true wealth we need comes straight from you
And bless us, Lord, with stillness, as we work throughout each day
When all these things we bring to you, dear Lord please hear us pray.